GREEK MYTHOLOGY

THE PRICE OF PANDORA

Graphic Planet
An Imprint of Magic Wagon
abdobooks.com

T0026256

THIS BOOK IS DEDICATED TO MY PARENTS CHARLES AND ROSE CAMPITI, WHO KNEW I COULD NEVER STOP READING. -DC

TO EVERYONE WHO LOVES A GREAT GREEK STORY ESPECIALLY MY CAT MIMITO. ILLUSTRATING THIS COLLECTION WAS CHALLENGING AND FUN. I LOVED THE WHOLE PROCESS. -LA

abdobooks.com

Printed in the United States of America, North Mankato, Minnesota.
102021
012022

THIS BOOK CONTAINS
RECYCLED MATERIALS

Written by David Campiti
Illustrated and Colored by Lelo Alves
Lettered by Kathryn S. Renta
Editorial Supervision by David Campiti/MJ Macedo
Packaged by Glass House Graphics
Research Assistance by Matt Simmons
Art Directed by Candice Keimig
Editorial Support by Tamara L. Britton

Library of Congress Control Number: 2020941566

Publisher's Cataloging-in-Publication Data

Names: Campiti, David, author. | Alves, Lelo, illustrator.
Title: The Price of Pandora / by David Campiti ; illustrated by Lelo Alves.
Description: Minneapolis, Minnesota : Magic Wagon, 2022. | Series: Greek mythology
Summary: Pandora unleashes horrible things in a graphic novel interpretation of this classic Greek myth.
Identifiers: ISBN 9781098231828 (lib. bdg.) | ISBN 9781644946640 (pbk.) | ISBN 9781098232382 (ebook) | ISBN 9781098232665 (Read-to-Me ebook)
Subjects: LCSH: Pandora (Greek mythological character)--Juvenile fiction. | Mythology, Greek--Juvenile fiction. | Gods, Greek--Juvenile fiction. | Heroes--Juvenile fiction. | Adventure stories--Juvenile fiction. | Graphic Novels--Juvenile fiction.
Classification: DDC 741.5--dc23

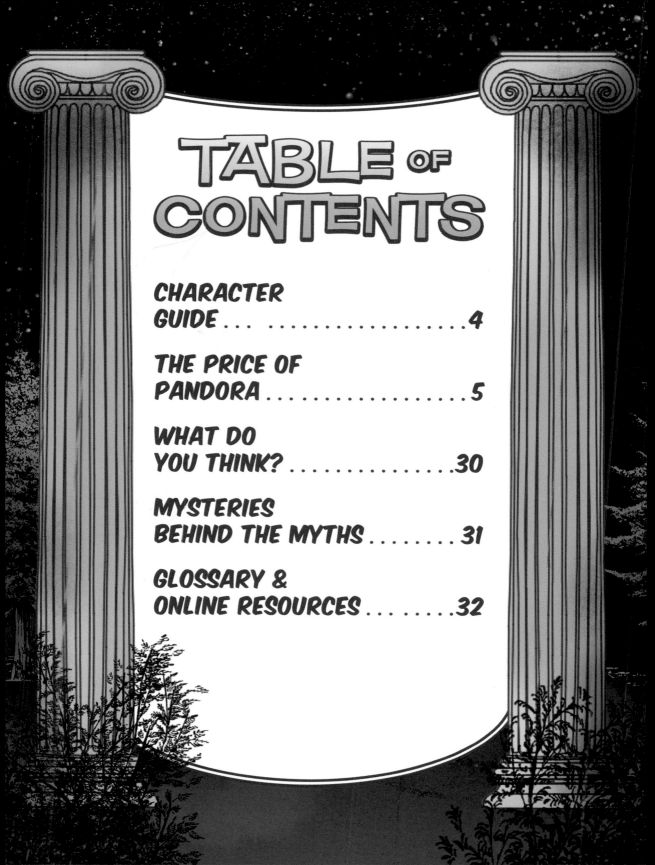

TABLE of CONTENTS

CHARACTER
GUIDE 4

THE PRICE OF
PANDORA 5

WHAT DO
YOU THINK? 30

MYSTERIES
BEHIND THE MYTHS 31

GLOSSARY &
ONLINE RESOURCES 32

CHARACTER GUIDE

HERMES
TRICKSTER & FLEET MESSENGER

PROMETHEUS
THINKING MAN'S TITAN

CHAOS
THE VOID

GAIA
ANCESTRAL EARTH MOTHER

PYRRHA
DAUGHTER OF EPIMETHEUS AND PANDORA

EPIMETHEUS
TITAN AFTERTHINKER

CRONUS
TITAN RULER

ZEUS
KING OF THE GODS

HEPHAESTUS
GOD OF BLACKSMITHS

PANDORA
FIRST HUMAN WOMAN

APHRODITE
GODDESS OF LOVE

ATHENA
GODDESS OF WARFARE & WISDOM

THAT'S WHEN CHAOS, IN HER INFINITE LONELINESS, CREATED EARTH'S MOTHER GAIA, WHO SPAWNED THE GROUND AND OCEANS AND HAD 12 TITANS AS CHILDREN.

TWO OF THEM GAVE BIRTH TO FOUR BROTHERS -- PROMETHEUS, EPIMETHEUS, MENOETIUS, AND ATLAS.

THERE CAME A TIME WHEN ZEUS WAGED WAR AGAINST HIS FATHER CRONUS FOR SUPREMACY. WHILE MOST TITANS SIDED WITH CRONUS --

-- PROMETHEUS BELIEVED ZEUS WOULD BE VICTORIOUS AND SIDED WITH HIM, BRINGING HIS BROTHER EPIMETHEUS WITH HIM.

WITH ALL THEIR CUNNING AND STRENGTH, THEY HELPED ZEUS WIN THE LONG, TERRIBLE BATTLE THAT FOLLOWED.

9

RATHER THAN LEARN FROM HIS FLAWED CHOICE AS THE TITAN HAD HOPED, ZEUS BECAME EVER MORE CONTEMPTFUL OF MEN.

PROMETHEUS BELIEVED THAT THE MEN WERE BEING UNDULY PUNISHED --

-- FOR A MISTAKE THAT WAS NEVER THEIRS BUT HIS BROTHER'S... AND HIS OWN.

SO PROMETHEUS STOLE FIRE FROM OLYMPIA'S SACRED FIREPIT TO GIVE TO MAN --

-- AND HIS MOST SELFLESS ACT WOULD BE HIS UNDOING.

HAHAHA! LIFE IS GOOD, MY BROTHER! I TAKE ALL THAT LIFE GIVES US!

JUST DO NOT TAKE ANY GIFTS FROM ZEUS!

HE WILL BE WRATHFUL, NOT FORGIVING!

SURE ENOUGH, ZEUS WOULD SOON MAKE AN EXAMPLE OF PROMETHEUS FOR HIS BETRAYAL.

PROMETHEUS, BOUND TO A CLIFF AS AN EAGLE ATE AWAY HIS LIVER, WHICH WOULD REGENERATE COME MORNING --

-- ONLY TO BE DEVOURED AGAIN AND AGAIN FOR ALL ETERNITY.

PANDORA SET LOOSE ALL THE EVILS ONTO THE WORLD, JUST AS ZEUS HAD ORDAINED.

OF COURSE SHE DID. ZEUS HAD MADE CERTAIN OF THAT.

OH, NO -- !

NO!!

IT WAS A CRUEL JOKE, ZEUS'S INFINITE JEST --

-- PLAYED OUT TO WICKED PERFECTION.

25

FOR THE BRIEFEST OF MOMENTS, PANDORA LAUGHS -- UNSURE OF WHY.

SLAMM

EMOTIONS FLOOD HER, AND SHE SUDDENLY KNOWS WHAT SHE HAS UNLEASHED INTO THE WORLD.

SHE CRIES FOR THE CHILD SHE DREAMS TO HAVE AND FOR THOSE ALL AROUND HER.

SO COLD -- !

THE EVILS UNLEASHED ARE SILENT, INVISIBLE, WITH NO WAY TO FEND THEM OFF.

→COUGH COUGH←

PANDORA, WHAT HAVE YOU DONE? YOU'VE OPENED THE JAR! YOU DEFIED ZEUS HIMSELF!

I COULD NOT HELP MYSELF.

I HAD TO KNOW WHAT WAS INSIDE.

I'M SO SORRY, MY HUSBAND!

WHAT HAPPENED NEXT IS A MYSTERY FOR THE AGES.

WAS THE ANSWER WORTH IT, MY LOVE?

HOW COULD IT BE?

IT WAS ZEUS'S REVENGE ON YOU -- AND ON ALL MEN!

SOME SAY PANDORA CLOSED THE BOX IN TIME FOR HOPE TO REMAIN INSIDE, SO THAT MAN WOULD NEVER LOSE HOPE.

OTHERS SAY THAT HOPE DID ESCAPE THE BOX, AND IT WAS THE MOST RUTHLESS EVIL OF ALL.

FOR HOPE IS WHAT MAKES MEN BELIEVE IN THINGS LONG AFTER THOSE THINGS ARE GONE. INSTEAD OF MOVING ON, MEN FALL INTO DESPAIR, CLINGING TO WHAT WILL NEVER BE.

DID HOPE ESCAPE? DID HOPE REMAIN? I WAS NOT THERE, SO I CANNOT SAY.

PANDORA DID HAVE A DAUGHTER AND WENT ON TO POPULATE THE WORLD.

YOU, OF COURSE, ARE ONE OF HER DESCENDANTS.

PYRRHA, I LOVE YOU SO!

SHE IS LOVELY, LIKE HER MOTHER.

AS FOR ME? I BREATHED INTO PANDORA SUCH FIERY CURIOSITY.

I GAVE IT HOPE AND DELIVERED THE JAR INTO PANDORA'S HANDS.

WHAT DO YOU THINK?

1. Myths tell of great gods, each of whom had special abilities and powers. However, they were as flawed as any human beings. What can you learn from the gods' behaviors in this story of Pandora?

2. Myths were passed down from generation to generation. They changed with each retelling. What tales of their childhoods have your parents and grandparents told? If they've told their stories more than once, did they embellish the stories to make them more entertaining? Have you told a story about something you did, where you changed the story in its retelling? Why?

3. Versions of the Greek myths have been told, retold, and adapted many times over the centuries. What other Greek myths have you read? What are your favorites, and why?

4. Myths of various gods are present in our everyday lives. Planets in our solar system, sailing ships, NASA spacecraft, cities, and various products are named after them. What are some you can remember?

5. Long before current religions, mankind conceived of gods and goddesses to explain mysterious happenings they did not understand. Different cultures told of different groups of gods. But those gods often matched up. For example, the Greek god Zeus was Odin to the Norse and Jupiter to the Romans. Aphrodite was Freyja to the Norse and Venus to the Romans. Do you know the matching names of any other gods, goddesses, or titans?

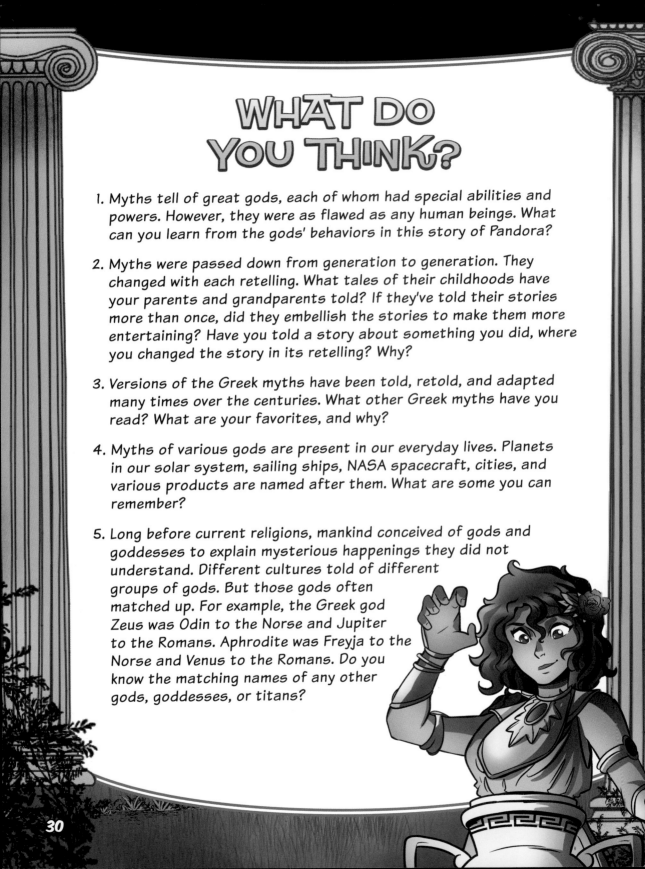

MYSTERIES BEHIND THE MYTHS

1. Were you surprised to learn that "Pandora's Box" was actually a jar in the original myth? In Hesiod's original Greek, the word was *pithos*, which was a large storage jar. When the tale was translated into Latin in the 16th century, *pithos* became *pyxis*, which means casket. That was later simplified to box. The myth has been retold as "Pandora's Box" ever since.

2. The custom of a dowry — a transfer of gifts, money, or property at a daughter's marriage — continues to this day. Unlike Zeus's cruel plan, a dowry is wealth intended to benefit the bride in her married life.

3. According to her myth, Zeus created Pandora as the first human woman, introduced into paradise. Some modern religions refer to the first woman as Eve, introduced into the Garden of Eden.

4. The person who wrote down the first version of Pandora's story is not known. However, around 700 BCE, the Greek poet Hesiod wrote an 828-line poem teaching his brother Perses about the agricultural arts. It included the story of Pandora, which endures today.

5. According to legend, not only was Hermes a confidant to the other gods and Zeus's errand boy, he periodically lived among the humans. He gauged their kindness and generosity for centuries after Pandora set loose evils upon the world, possibly as penance for the part he played in punishing humanity.

GLOSSARY

APHRODITE — Goddess of love, beauty, and passion. Married to the god Hephaestus.

ATHENA — Goddess of handicraft, warfare, and wisdom. Daughter of Zeus and the goddess Metis.

CHAOS — The vast void at the dawn of time, which gave form to Erebus (darkness), Eros (desire), Gaia (earth), Tartarus (the abyss), and Nyx (night), the foundations of the universe.

CRONUS — Direct descendant of Gaia (earth) and Uranus (sky), ruler and youngest of the first generation of Titans. He and the goddess Rhea were parents of Chiron, Demeter, Hades, Hera, Hestia, and Zeus.

EPIMETHEUS — Titan, the "afterthinker," who could only see his mistakes after he made them. The excitable, foolish brother of Prometheus.

GAIA — The personification of earth, considered the ancestral mother of all life. From her came the Cyclopes, the Giants, and the Titans.

GREECE — A mountainous country with many islands, located on the Mediterranean Sea. Considered the birthplace of democracy and early mathematical and scientific principles and the place from which the gods ruled.

HEPHAESTUS — God of blacksmiths, stonework, and technology, devoted son of Zeus and Hera. Considered the least attractive of the gods, yet married to the beautiful Aphrodite.

HERMES — The divine trickster, son of Zeus and Maia, the emissary and fleet messenger of the gods. He even conducted souls into the afterlife.

HORAE — These were goddesses of the seasons of nature, named Auxo, Carpo, and Thallo.

MOUNT OLYMPUS — A real mountain in Thessaly, Greece, towering nearly 9,800 feet (2,987 m) above the sea. This is the site around which the mythology for the gods was created.

OLYMPIA — The fabled city that the gods inhabited and from which Zeus ruled, located at the top of Mount Olympus.

PANDORA — The "all-gifted" first human woman, created by Hephaestus at Zeus's direction. Imbued with overwhelming curiosity, she became Zeus's vessel to open the jar that delivered deceit, evil, and sickness to punish humanity.

PROMETHEUS — A Titan with intelligence and forethought, usually considering the consequences an action or decision might bring. He tricked and stole from Zeus to champion mankind, and in so doing suffered Zeus's wrath.

TITANS — The twelve children of first-ever parents Gaia and Uranus. Their loyalties split in the great war, the Titanomachy, in which Zeus overthrew his father Cronus for supremacy.

ZEUS — God of lightning, son of Cronus and Rhea, husband to Hera. He fought a great and terrible war to become King of the gods of Olympus.

ONLINE RESOURCES

Booklinks
NONFICTION NETWORK
FREE! ONLINE NONFICTION RESOURCES

To learn more about **GREEK MYTHOLOGY**, visit **abdobooklinks.com** or scan this QR code. These links are routinely monitored and updated to provide the most current information available.